# Perfect Score The SAT

A detailed guide for obtaining a
perfect score on the SAT

# Author's Note

Hello Reader,

I first took the SAT November of my junior year. I had studied for it for two years, and it was a great pleasure when the perfect 2400 came in. Since then, I've tutored over thirty students using my methods, with an average score improvement of over 230 points. One lucky junior even had his score go up 470 points. Another student also managed to match my 2400. My curriculum is proven to get results.

The core of my tutoring curriculum is centered on writing using proper structure, learning grammar rules, memorizing vocabulary, and practicing math problems. I designed my unique SAT Essay Structure after studying dozens of full score essays, and mixing in my own innovations. The Grammar section contains all the rules that are normally discussed in SAT preparation, plus the rarer ones that I ran across while taking dozens of practice SATs. The SAT vocabulary list I compiled and memorized allowed me to go through entire reading sections without ever needing to use the process of elimination—I knew the denotations and connotations of every word. And the math section too, is quite extensive.

All of this information is provided here, enough to give anyone with a reasonable amount of time a decent shot at obtaining a 2400. Even with just 10 weeks, considerable progress can be made. As I stated before, my average student improved over 230 points after spending 10 sessions with me. There's something for everyone here, so go and get started!

Dan Chen

# Table of Contents

# Chapter 1: The Perfect Score Method

## What Not To Do

The next time you take an exam, be it the SAT, a midterm, or simply a major test, take a look at the people around you. Not at their answers of course, but the students themselves—more specifically, at their abdomens.

That's right, at their abdomens. Normally, everyone breathes with his or her diaphragm, an action that causes the stomach to inflate and deflate. However, one of the most common test taking errors is that people actually forget to breathe. Their shoulders shrug up and down as they subconsciously gulp in little gasps of breath from time to time. They do not use their diaphragms, and their abdomens stay perfectly still. This causes a variety of problems, such as reduced focus, increased proclivity to rush, and a general sense of nervousness. Try not to do this. And so the next time you take a test, take a look around at your peers. A sea of frozen stomachs will tell you that on one of the most basic levels possible, just about everyone taking the test is at a disadvantage to you.

There are a variety of other mistakes to avoid, and much of the rest of this book will revolve around helping you identify them. You'll pick up a variety of techniques, some old and almost instinctive, others fresh and unorthodox. But the most important aspect is to get practice. This book alone won't get you a perfect score—it needs to be combined with dozens and dozens of hours doing problems and practice tests.

So, the very simple lesson of this passage is: Don't forget to breath, don't forget to practice. There, one lesson down, many more to go.

# Strategy

The book is designed so that you can study at your pace. Perhaps you're a freshman trying to get a head start what is likely the most important test of your high school career. With that much time, you should definitely aim for that 2400. Or perhaps you've got 10 weeks before your SAT. Then, consult the approach outlined in Chapter 5. This approach is the written form of my one-to-one tutoring program, and has averaged over 230 points of improvement per student. No matter how much time you have, you will be able to benefit significantly from this book.

The core of my tutoring curriculum is centered around writing using proper structure, learning grammar rules, memorizing vocabulary, and practicing-practicing-practicing math problems. The 16 rules of SAT grammar will give you no excuse to miss any writing section multiple choice questions. The proper Four-Paragraph structure will ensure that you can come up with an organized and clear essay no matter how strange the question. My vocabulary lists are compilations of the most ubiquitous and useful SAT vocabulary words. But to master the lessons in this book requires practice—outside practice. This book should be supplemented with additional practice SATs, available on the CollegeBoard website and from practice test compilation books. My own 2400 was achieved by completing over two dozen self-administered practice tests. At 3 hours per test, (a conservative estimate) that is over 70 hours of just taking the SAT. Always remember to practice.

With sufficient time and practice, anyone can have a reasonable chance at obtaining a perfect score on the SAT. The following chapter goes through the necessary facts and techniques to significantly improve your potential.

# Chapter 2: Writing

## The Essay

The first section you will encounter on the SAT is the essay. The key to being able to consistently write a high scoring essay is Structure. Always follow the Structure. Once you have written half a dozen essays using the Structure, you will never again be pressed for time, and never again be at a loss for words.

### The Structure:

First, we start by brainstorming. You may have a negative schema of the word "brainstorm," from 7t\h grade English class, but brainstorming for the SAT is a much simpler matter. Instead of creating coherent sentences for your English teacher to correct, you are now truly thinking for yourself. That means no complete sentences, no explanations, no introductions or conclusions. You merely write down 4 words to summarize your two supporting examples for the essay.

Let's say that our essay topic is "Does history repeat itself?" For brainstorming, I would simply write down *"Holocaust Libya, Depression Recession."* What does that mean? It means that my first example will be on how the Holocaust did not repeat itself in Libya, and my second example will be on how the Great Depression did not repeat itself during the Great Recession. That will be it as far as brainstorming goes. Simple, right?

Next we move to the introduction. The introduction should always start with a hook: a broad, general statement about the world in general. So going back to our "Does history repeat itself" example, I would start my essay with,

*"Although on the surface history may appear as a cyclical wheel of time, deeper examination reveals that humans do learn from the mistakes of their ancestors."*

Follow that with a brief summary of your two examples as development for your introduction. The key here is to present them in a casual manner. In this case, I would try to relate the two examples together in a single sentence.

*"Through government intervention, the Holocaust did not repeat itself in Libya, and the Great Depression did not repeat itself during the Great Recession.*

After summarizing your examples, finish off your introduction paragraph with your thesis statement. It should be a firm, biased declaration of your unwavering support, regardless of whether or not you truly feel so polarized on the matter. Remember that this is not a persuasive essay: you do not have to acknowledge and refute the counterpoint. In fact, taking the time to do so will only weaken your essay. Therefore, try to avoid mentioning the counterpoint altogether. If you cannot resist the urge, please limit yourself to just a single sentence on addressing the opposing view.

*"Humanity learns from its mistakes; where education thrives, history does not manage to repeat itself."*

Putting it all together gives us a riveting introduction paragraph.

*Although on the surface history may appear as a cyclical wheel of time, deeper examination reveals that humans do learn from the mistakes of their ancestors. Through government interventions, the Holocaust did not repeat itself in Libya, and the Great Depression did not repeat itself during the Great Recession. Humanity learns from its mistakes; where education thrives, history does not manage to repeat itself.*

Next we move on to the first body paragraph. It should start by tying your first example to your thesis. Always lead with the example, as it demonstrates that your essay is organized, and that you have something interesting to say.

*Germany in 1939 resembled Libya in 2011in a variety of ways, but in Libya, no genocides were committed.*

Follow this up by qualifying your example with supporting details.

*Both countries were under the rule of power-crazed dictators, and both countries had militaries far superior to any resistance the citizens could have put up. Germany's Hitler used this superiority to massacre the "unwanted" of his Reich. Libya's Gaddafi tried to do the same. But unlike in Nazi Germany, the world stepped in to stop Gaddafi's madness. U.N. planes decimated Gaddafi's tanks and European weapons flowed into the hands of Libyan rebels. The world gleaned from the Holocaust the price of apathy, and did not allow genocide in Libya.*

And that concludes your first body paragraph. Now repeat for your second example. The only new thing to keep in mind this time around is to make sure the first sentence of your second body paragraph has some sort of transition in it.

*Economic failures also do not tend to lend themselves to repetition. Historians and economists agree that the Great Depression was partially fueled by the fact that the government had cut spending tremendously once times started getting rough; with this in mind, the Obama administration opened up the floodgates of government spending once the Great Recession started. With massive bailouts and an unprecedented 0% interest rate, the Obama administration pumped massive amounts of cash into the American economy. As a result, the Great Recession did not turn into the Great Depression. By learning from the mistakes of the past, the government managed to avoid repeating the errors of previous administrations.*

With your two examples complete, we now move to the conclusion. Yes, that means there will only be 4 paragraphs. That however, does not violate any rules of writing. The 5-paragraph format you learned about in middle school is designed for 45-minute expository or persuasive responses—using it for the SAT will only put you at risk for creating examples with insufficient detail. The 4-paragraph format is better for the SAT.

So what goes into the last paragraph? The conclusion should include a restatement of your two examples. It also should finish with another broad and general statement related to your thesis. Remember that since SAT essays are graded holistically, the graders are not looking too carefully at the ending. All you need to do is to finish with some semblance of a coherent and well-learned being to earn that perfect score.

*History has shown us that humans do learn from our errors. Whether it is understanding the consequences of failing to come to our brothers' aid, or recognizing the economics blunders of the past, people and governments do learn. Libya did not turn into another Nazi Germany, and The Great Recession is not another Great Depression. The astounding human capacity for learning ensures that mistakes of the past serve as warnings and cautions to the present.*

And there we have it: a perfect SAT essay.

*Although on the surface history may appear as a cyclical wheel of time, deeper examination reveals that humans do learn from the mistakes of their ancestors. Through government intervention, the Holocaust did not repeat itself in Libya, and the Great Depression did not repeat itself during the Great Recession. Humanity learns from its mistakes; where education thrives, history does not manage to repeat itself.*

*Germany in 1940 resembled Libya in 2011 in a variety of ways, but in Libya, no genocides were committed. Both countries were under the rule of power-crazed dictators, and both countries had militaries far superior to any resistances the citizens could have put up. Germany's Hitler used this superiority to massacre the "unwanted" of his Reich. Libya's Gaddafi tried to do the same. But unlike in Nazi Germany, the world stepped in to stop the dictator's madness. U.N. planes decimated Gaddafi's tanks and European weapons flowed into the hands of Libyan rebels. The world gleaned from the Holocaust the price of apathy, and did not allow another genocide in Libya.*

*Economic failures also do not easily lend themselves to repetition. Historians and economists agree that the Great Depression of the 1930s was partially fueled by the fact that the government had cut spending tremendously once times started getting rough; with this in mind, the Obama administration opened up the floodgates of government spending once the Great Recession started. With massive bailouts and an unprecedented 0% interest rate, the Obama administration pumped massive amounts of cash into the American economy. As a result, the Great Recession did not worsen into another Great Depression. By learning from the mistakes of the past, the government managed to avoid repeating the errors of previous administrations.*

*History has shown us that humans do learn from our errors. Whether it is understanding the consequences of failing to come to our brothers' aid, or recognizing the economics blunders of inexperienced administrations, people and governments do learn. Libya did not turn into another Nazi Germany, and The Great Recession is not another Great Depression. The astounding human capacity for learning ensures that mistakes of the past serve as warnings and cautions to the present.*

So, to recap, the structure you should use exclusively now for SAT essays is as thus:

1) Plan your two examples using approximately 4 words
2) Start your introduction with a hook
3) Summarize your two examples
4) Finish your introduction with a firm thesis statement.
5) Start body paragraph 1 by stating how example 1 ties in with your thesis.
6) Qualify and explain example 1
7) Start body paragraph 2 with a transition
8) Explain how example 2 ties in with your thesis.
9) Qualify and explain example 2
10) Summarize your two examples in the conclusion
11) Finish your essay with a broad statement about humanity in general.

Of course, practice is vital to master this Structure. I would start by writing 2 essays every weekend. In the month before you take the exam, move that number up to 5 or more. Practice makes perfect! And practice also makes sure you can properly manage your time and essay length.

Speaking of essay length, note that almost all perfect essays have 1 aspect in common: they are long. Length does not ensure a high score, but it is necessary for properly supporting your examples. Try to keep your essays above the 300-word mark.

And there you have it, SAT essay writing in a nutshell. Memorizing the structure and practicing it will guarantee you the perfect first section of your SAT.

# Hierarchy of Example Choice

So how do we pick examples to use for our essay? Well, make sure your topic is something that you know well and have accurate information on. Then, consult the Hierarchy of Example Choice.

On the top of the hierarchy are **historical examples**. Graders love a bit of history in your essay. Talk about the wars and events discussed in your American History or Comparative Cultures class. As long as you can provide adequate and correct information you will have great success with historical examples.

Coming in close to first place are **biographical examples**. Graders also love to hear a real human's story. Note that only famous and respected figures should be used here. Abraham Lincoln is okay, the celebrity from that new reality TV show is not. Also, if you want to discuss Gandhi, please spell his name correctly. Every few months one of my students will tell me about the sacrifices made by his personal hero "Ghandi."

**Current Events** oftentimes are very useful in dealing with essay prompt about current issues. A relevant and recent war, economics crisis, or scientific discovery can help drive your essay's point home.

**Literary examples** and **literary quotes** reside lower in the hierarchy. Used properly, they can perfectly support your point. However, since you only have 25 minutes to write, perhaps you should try to make sure as much of your material comes from your own mind as possible.

**Personal Anecdotes** at times can be effective for the SAT essay, but more often are not. Unfortunately, most people just do not have that interesting or credible of a story to tell. Try to avoid personal anecdotes.

On the bottom of the hierarchy are **generic ideas**. Try to avoid using generic ideas for the SAT essay. If you want to write about friendship, pick the friendship of two literary characters instead. If you want to write about extradition, pick a famous political refugee instead of saying extradition is philosophically immoral. Do not use vague examples.

So, as a general rule:

## Historical examples > Biographical examples > Current event examples > Literary examples > Personal Anecdotes > Generic ideas

When selecting your examples for you SAT essay, it is best to keep this Hierarchy of Example Choice in mind.

# Sample Prompts

1) We are oftentimes forced to conform to society's standards, sometimes for the better, sometimes for the worse. Is being true to yourself a challenge in modern society?

2) All men, great and mediocre, have made mistakes in life. What is the relationship between mistakes and creativity?

3) Failure is an unavoidable part of life. How can we use failure to improve?

4) Privacy is a fiercely debated topic in today's society. Are security cameras in public places an invasion of privacy?

5) Some people say that we should never infringe upon freedom. Others say that we freedom is secondary when pursuing the greater good. Are there situations in which we should restrict freedom for the greater good?

6) Many of us let go of our fantasies and daydreams as we grow older. But do we need fantasy and nonsense in daily life?

7) Can money produce happiness?

8) Public education is a fiercely debated issue in the United States. How can a teacher best affect his or her students?

9) The government is present in our daily lives; if we want to buy a car we must also buy car insurance, if we want to open a business we need

to register with the state. Should the government sponsor such initiatives to control the daily actions of ordinary citizens?

10) Genetically modified foods are starting to fill the shelves of our stores. Should government pass laws requiring labels for genetically modified foods?

11) America's top athletes oftentimes make millions of dollars every year. Do you think professional athletes deserve their high salaries?

12) Some say that if we can help the poor with little bother to ourselves, we are obliged to do so. Others say that helping the poor is completely voluntary, and refraining from doing does not make us immoral people. Is giving to the poor a moral obligation for those of us with money to spare?

13) Technology has brought into the world a higher standard of living for billions. It has also brought into the world new capacities for creating human suffering. Does technology help or hurt society more?

14) Nowadays, we can learn much from the Internet. However, some say this method of learning is not comparable to a traditional education. Can online schools provide quality training and a legitimate degree?

15) The government requires parents to provide their children the basic amenities of life, such as food and shelter. However, parents can decide to deprive their children of other amenities, such as vaccinations. Should parents be required to provide medical care to their children?

16) In the wake of an increase media focus on school shootings, many schools are stationing police officers on school grounds. Is having a police presence in schools an acceptable facet of society?

# Grammar

Chances are, you have been exposed to a bevy of grammatical errors from a multifaceted array of sources while growing up. Let us try a quick exercise: identify which of the following phrases and sentences are incorrect.

1) None of the people here are fit to lead.
2) This line is for customer with 10 items or less.
3) I'm worried for you.
4) This is just between you and I.
5) The girls flouted their dresses.
6) At the funeral, everybody paid their respects.

Guess what? They're all wrong. Now can you tell me why? If you cannot, do not worry! After learning my 16 rules of SAT Grammar, you will be able to identify why each and every one of them is incorrect.

By the way, here are the error types in the previous sentences. Take a look and refer to the grammar rules for more information.

1) Subject verb agreement error
2) Quantitative vs. Qualitative error
3) Prepositional error
4) Idiomatic error
5) Spelling error
6) Subject Pronoun Agreement error

# 1) Adjectives vs. adverbs

**The Rule**: adjectives are used to modify nouns, adverbs are used to modify verbs.

**Correct Usage**: The clever fox quickly jumped over the lazy dog

"Clever" is an adjective that modifies the noun "fox" ; "quickly" is an adverb that modifies the verb "jumped" ; "lazy" is an adjective that modifies the noun "dog."

**Incorrect Usage:**

*The cleverly fox.*
The adverb "cleverly" cannot describe the noun "fox"

*The fox jumped over quick.*
The adjective "quick" cannot describe the verb "jumped"

*I performed good.*
The adjective "good" cannot describe the verb jumped.

Note that "well" is an adverb and "good" is an adjective. So it would be correct to say "The dog felt well," or "The dog was good." It would be incorrect to say "The dog ran good," or "The well dog was here."

## 2) Clarity

**The Rule**: Pronouns need a clear subject.

**Correct usage**: Marty was sad; he did not feel well. John was also sad; he felt badly about Marty's sadness.

We know that the first pronoun "he" refers to the subject "Marty", and the second pronoun "he" refers to the subject "John."

**Incorrect Usage:** Marty told John that he was sad.

In this sentence, who is sad? It could be either Marty or John. Therefore it is not clear what subject the pronoun "he" is referring to.

## 3) Comparisons: 2 subjects vs. 2+ Subjects

Different words are used to compare subjects. You would not say "Between Joe and Jill, Joe is the best," but rather, "Between Joe and Jill, Joe is better." A table is used to illustrate some other words that follow this rule.

| Two Subjects | More than Two Subjects |
|---|---|
| Between: "This secret is between you and me." | Among: "We will share this sandwich among the three of us." |
| Greater: "7 is greater than '6'." | Greatest: "Of the three numbers, '8' is the greatest." |
| Less: "I like bacon less than ham" | Least: "Among bacon, ham, and fish, I like fish the least" |
| Better: "Cars are better than buses." | Best: "Among cars, boats and bikes, bikes are the best mode of transportation. |

Using a word meant for two subjects when there are three subjects present, and vice versa, will result in a grammatical error.

## 4) Comparisons: Subjects Vs. Possessions

**The Rule:** Owners can be compared to other owners, and possessions can be compared to other possessions, but owners cannot be compared to their possessions.

**Correct Usage**: Tolkien's book is better than Kafka's book

We compare the possession "book" to another book.

**Incorrect Usage**: Stephanie's book is better than Rowling.

We are comparing a possession "book" to an owner, "Rowling."

## 5) Implied Comparisons

**The Rule**: Sometimes when using a comparison, there are "implied words."

**Incorrect Usage**: "Jake is more athletic than me."

You may think that "me" is being properly used as an object pronoun. However, the sentence is incorrect.

**Correct Usage**: "Jake is more creative than I."

Why is this correct? Because "I" in this case implies "I am." So the sentence, "Jake is more creative than I" is actually saying, "Jake is more creative than I am." That is the proper comparison.

## 6) Independent Clauses

**The Rule:** 2 independent clauses in a sentence must be joined by a semicolon or a conjunction--not a comma, and not the word, "however." (Because "however" is not a conjunction)

**Correct Usage**: Ray will go to the bank and he will go to swim practice. Justin will go to the bank; he will go to swim practice.

There are two independent clauses in the first sentence, "Ray will go to the bank," and "he will go to swim practice." They are properly joined by the conjunction "and." There are two independent clauses in the second sentence, "Justin will go to the bank," and "he will go to swim practice." they are properly joined by a semicolon.

**Incorrect Usage**: Ray will go to the bank, he will go to swim practice. Justin will go to the bank, however, he will go to swim practice first.

In the first sentence, there are two independent clauses, but they are incorrectly joined by a comma. In the second sentence, there are two independent clauses, but they are improperly joined by the word, "however." Both instances create run on sentences, and are incorrect.

## 7) Modifiers

**The Rule**: A phrase that describes is a modifier. The subject that the modifier describes needs to come directly after the modifying phrase.

**Correct Usage**: Known for producing some of the best literature the world has ever seen, J.K. Rowling is a British writer.

In this sentence, the modifier is "Known for producing some of the best literature the world has ever seen." The subject it describes, J.K. Rowling, comes directly after the modifying phrase.

**Incorrect Usage**: Known for producing some of the best literature in the world, the Harry Potter books were written by J.K. Rowling.

In this sentence, the modifier is "Known for producing some of the best literature in the world." This phrase is meant to describe J.K. Rowling. However, by having, "The Harry Potter books" be placed directly after the modifier, the sentence is altered to mean that the Harry Potter books produced some of the best literature in the world. The misplaced subject completely changes the meaning of the sentence, and is incorrect.

## 8) Parallelism

**The Rule:** Verbs in a list need to take the same form.

**Correct usage**: The British spy team was expected to run, to jump, and to climb.

In this sentence, the verbs "run", "jump", and "climb" are all in the same form. They are parallel and grammatically correct.

**Incorrect Usage**: The American spy team was expected to help, to assist, and providing support.

In this sentence, the verbs "help", "assist", and "provide" are not in the same form. They are not parallel and thus grammatically incorrect.

In addition, pronoun shifts within a sentence also disobeys the rule of parallelism. When writing about the things that "you" will do, don't suddenly switch instead to writing about the things that "one" will do.

## 9) Prepositions

A preposition is simply a word that demonstrates the relationship between two words. Some examples are "about", "before", "beyond", "despite", and "without". Prepositions do not follow a given set of rules. Instead, they follow idiomatic use.

Often, there are multiple correct prepositions to use with prepositions. For example, Back Up, Back Down, and Back away are all correct, and each of them uses a different preposition with the verb back. There are a few common errors with prepositions though.

**Incorrect Usage:**

Ex 1: Worried about: Never use the phrase "worried for." Perhaps you have heard it used in common day language. However, it is grammatically incorrect. I am worried about you, not for you.

Ex. 2: Hit over: The phrase, "hit over the head" is a colloquial expression--but not a grammatically correct one.

Ex 3: Ending a sentence: Prepositions are usually not used to end a sentence. "The lot is where I park my car in" ends with the preposition "in" and is incorrect. However, exceptions to the rule exist, such as the grammatically correct, "I turn the radio on." The general rule here is to not use extraneous prepositions at the end of sentences.

Ex. 4: "like" vs. "such as." "Like" is always used for comparisons; when you want to introduce a list of items, use "such as" instead.

Ex 5: who, where, when. "Who" always refers to a person, "where" always refers to a location, and "when" refers to an occurrence or a time period.

Finally, use common sense to weed out prepositions used in the incorrect context of a sentence. When a sentence looks like gibberish, like "the sexist boss discriminated into hiring females." you should be able to identify that it is incorrect.

## 10) Proper Tense

**The Rule**: Verbs need to be consistent in tense in a phrase.

**Correct Usage**: The Romans of the Golden Age shaved everyday of the week but never bathed.

In this sentence, "shaved", and "bathed" are both in the past tense. This is grammatically correct.

**Incorrect Usage**: In Ancient Egypt, the servants had feared cats and believed superstitions.

"Fear" and "believed" are in different tenses. Since the setting is Ancient Egypt, the verbs have both been in the past tense. To correct the error, use, "The servants feared cats and believed superstitions."

# 11) Quantitative vs Qualitative Comparisons

We have all heard that supermarkets using the sign "10 Items or Less" are spreading a grammatical error. There are a few more errors like it.

| Quantitative | Qualitative |
|---|---|
| Fewer: I ate fewer burgers to lose weight | Less: I used less ketchup to lose weight |
| Many: I ate many burgers because I was hungry | Much: I used much more ketchup than was needed |
| Number: I own a large number of fast food restaurants. | Amount: I have a tremendous amount of ketchup on my burger. |

Using these the other way around produces errors.

**Incorrect Usage:**

Example 1) I use less napkins to cut down on waste.

Napkins can be counted, and are quantitative. "Fewer" is used with quantitative nouns.

Example 2) North Korea has many more happiness than South Korea.

Happiness cannot be counted and is qualitative. "Much" is used with qualitative nouns.

Example 3) The amount of payments we make to the landlord is too high.

Payments can be counted and is quantitative. "Number" is used with quantitative nouns.

## 12) Spelling

Error ID questions occasionally provide some misspelled words for you to catch. They have become far less common in the more recent versions of the SAT. However, here are some common spelling traps from the past.

Commonly confused word pairs:

a) Flout vs. Flaunt: The first means "to disobey"; the second means "to show off."

b) Flair vs. Flare: The first means "style"; the second is what you shoot into the air to signal for rescue ships.

c) Eminent vs. imminent: The first means "famous"; the second means "about to arrive."

d) Condone vs. condemn: The first means "to endorse"; the second means "to hate."

e) Effect vs. affect: The first is a noun; the second is a verb

f) Vain vs. vein: The expression "In this vein" cannot be used with "vain."

g) Complement vs. compliment: The first means "to make whole"; the second means "to praise."

h) Canvass vs. canvas: The first means "to examine"; the second is material used for painting.

i) Allude vs. elude: The first means "to refer to"; the second means "to avoid."

## 13) Subject Possession agreement

**The Rule**: Subjects and their possessions need to agree in plurality.

**Correct Usage**: The captain told the pirates to put their hands up in the air.
In this sentence, the plural subject, "pirates" is paired with the plural possession, "hands." This is grammatically correct.

**Incorrect Usage**: Koalas, though known for being mindless and slow, are very protective of their cub.

In this sentence, the plural subject "Koalas" is paired with the singular possession "cub." Koalas have more than one cub! This pairing improperly conveys the meaning of the sentence.

## 14) Subject Pronouns vs. Object Pronouns

**The Rule**: There are two types of pronouns, subject pronouns and object pronouns. The general rule is that subject pronouns do things, and things are done onto or by object pronouns. More formally, subject pronouns use the Active voice, and object pronouns use the Passive voice.

| Subject Pronouns | Object Pronouns |
| --- | --- |
| I | Me |
| You | You |
| He | Him |
| She | Her |
| It | It |
| Who | Whom |
| We | Us |
| They | Them |

**Correct Usage**: "I write books. Books are written by me."

The first sentence uses the object pronoun "I" and is in the active voice. The second sentence uses the subject pronoun "me" and is in the passive voice.

**Incorrect Usage**: The book was written by he. Whom wrote the book?

The first sentence uses the subject pronoun "he," but is passive. To correct it, use the object pronoun "him." The book was written by him.

The second sentence uses the object pronoun "whom," but is active. Use the subject pronoun "who" to correct it.

**Note:** The active voice is considered "better" than the passive voice by SAT makers. If a question asks you for the BEST choice and you are down to two grammatically correct choices, always choose the one with active voice.

## 15) Subject Verb Agreement

**The Rule**: Singular subjects go with verbs that end in "s" and look plural. Plural subjects go with verbs that look singular.

**Correct Usage**: The apostles appear to be preaching. Jesus appears to be preaching too.

In the first sentence, the plural subject "apostles" is paired with the singular looking verb "appear." In the second sentence, the singular subject "Jesus" is paired with the plural looking verb "appears."

**Note**: Often, grammar books will tell you that verbs like "appear" are plural and verbs like "appears" are singular. Here I call verbs like "appear" singular-looking, and verbs like "appears" plural-looking. As long as you know how the verb is supposed to be used, it does not matter what you call it.

**Incorrect Usage**: The Crusaders from Jerusalem jumps on top of the hill. Richard appear to be leading them.

In the first sentence, the plural subject "Crusaders" is used with the plural looking verb "jumps." The verb "jump" should have been used instead.

In the second sentence, the singular subject "Richard" is used with the singular looking verb "appear." The verb "appears" should have been used instead.

Sometimes it is difficult to identify if a subject is singular or plural. Here's a list of some common singular subjects that are often misused.

None: None of the men is capable of defeating Chuck.
The United Nations: The United Nations is pretty cool.
Either: Either of them is suitable for the task.

Neither: Neither this rope nor that rope is strong enough to restrain the bear.

The United States: The United States is pretty cool as well.

Each: Each of us here is responsible for cleanup.

Anyone: Anyone is capable of doing the impossible.

Everyone: Everyone is capable of doing the impossible.

No One: No one is capable of defeating Chuck.

So the next time you hear someone saying "none of you are good enough," you'll be able to identify the subject-verb agreement error in his or her sentence.

Another sub-rule in subject verb agreement is that fractions and percentages cause plurality to depend on the noun.

**Correct Usage**: 90% of the turtles are green.

There is a percentage present, so we refer to the noun "turtles." Turtles are plural, and so "are" green.

**Incorrect Usage**: Over one half of the human body are water.

There is a fraction present, so we refer to the noun "human body." That is singular, therefore "is" water.

In addition, when 2 subjects are joined by "and," they are always plural.

**Correct Usage:** John and Jake are friends. The Jews and the Muslims are cool.

However, when 2 subjects are joined by "or," the **latter subject takes the plurality**. That means the second subject determines whether to use a singular or plural verb.

**Correct Usage**: John or the players are competing tomorrow.

The second subject is "players" and so "are" is used.


**Correct Usage:** The players or John is competing tomorrow.

The second subject is "John" and so "is" is used.

## 16) Subject Pronoun Agreement:

This rule builds on the rule on Subject-Verb agreement

**The Rule**: Subjects and their pronouns have to agree in plurality.

**Correct Usage**: Everyone was told to take his hat off.

In this sentence, the singular subject "everyone," is paired with the singular pronoun "his."

**Incorrect Usage**: Everyone was told that they were being rude.

In this sentence, the singular subject "everyone" is used with the plural pronoun "they." Singular subjects need to be paired with singular pronouns.

There you have it. 16 grammar rules that will help you master the SAT writing section. Now get in some practice!

# Grammar Drills

1) (a)Of the two (b)phones, I liked the blue (c)one the (d)best. (e)No error.

2) The storm (a)clouds indicated (b)clear that there (c)was a major storm (d)coming. (e)No error.

3) Throughout the (a)year, (b)tourists come to the Grand (c)Canyon to admire the scenery, experience the excitement, and (d)hiking to the best landmarks. (e)No error.

4) The (a)bass player told the (b)drummer that (c)he was an integral member of the (d)band. (e)No error.

5) (a) Jane was excited (b)because her fantasy (c)football team was better than (d)Justin. (e)No Error

6) Jonathan (a)is a world (b)famous painter and (c)therefore is more creative than (d)I. (e)No Error

7) Because (a)it was an intelligent animal, the (b)dog was (c)trusted with important (d)duties. (e)No Error

8) After (a)receiving (b)no answer from (c)Joey's phone, Mary became worried (d)for her friend. (e)No Error

9) (a)Though it is rare, (b)grammar questions on the exam sometimes (c)contain (d)no error. (e)No error.

10) In (a)medieval (b)times, children (c)go to school (d)only once in a week. (e)No Error

11) Patrick (a)vowed to eat (b)less hamburgers (c)so that he could lose (d)weight. (e)No Error

12) The (a)girls at the dance (b)flouted their (c)dresses and twirled on the (d)dance-floor. (e)No Error

13) Upon (a)hearing their captain's (b)voice, the (c)pirates put their (d)hand in the air and shouted. (e)No Error

14) The (a)engine check of the (b)van was performed by the (c)soldier and (d)him. (e)No Error

15) None of the (a)ships (b)are fit for (c)sailing, so we must stay here for (d)the night. (e)No Error

16) Everyone (a)was told to take (b)their hats off (c)upon entering (d)the building. (e)No Error

# Solutions

1. D) "Best" is used to compare more than two items. "Better" should have been used instead.

2. B) A classic adjective-adverb question. "clearly" would have been the correct answer.

3. D) This is a parallelism error.

4. C) It is unclear which musician "he" refers to.

5. D) This is a faulty comparison. The team should have been compared to "Justin's team."

6. E) There is no error in this sentence. Remember that in this scenario, "I" implies "I am"

7. E) No Error, the modifier was used correctly.

8. D) The proper preposition is "about."

9. E) There is no error in this sentence.

10. C) "Go" should be replaced with "went."

11. B) "Fewer" is used for quantitative items like hamburgers.

12. B) The proper word is "flaunted," not "flouted."

13. D) "Hands" should be used instead.

14. E) There is no error in this sentence.

15. B) "none" is singular.

16. B) "Everyone" is singular, and "their" is plural.

# Chapter 3: Reading

Reading is without a doubt the hardest section on the SAT to prepare for. Fortunately, you have lots of time and help to get ready.

First of all: read prolifically. Everything and anything you can get your hands on that has any sort of literary merit is fair game. My recommended Book List is filled with not only books of the English literary "canon", but fantasy, science fiction, and a variety of other enjoyable literature. You should attempt to finish the list if you are aiming for a perfect score.

Vocabulary is also crucial to success in critical reading. Every reading section starts with vocabulary, and while the process of elimination strategy is useful, it is far less effective than knowing the correct answer right off the bat. To aim for a 2400, you should definitely memorize my entire vocabulary list. And of course, to see those words used in actual passages and sentences, read my Book List.

Finally, to tackle the passages, there is also a bevy of rules and strategies. We'll get to those too.

# Readings List

Here are a few readings you can enjoy and learn SAT vocabulary from at the same time.

*1984* by George Orwell: Ever wish you could read science fiction in English class? *1984* is your answer. It's part of the literary canon, and also has a riveting storyline.

*A Farewell to Arms* by Ernest Hemingway: The vocabulary is a bit basic in this novel, but it's still firmly entrenched in the literary canon.

*A Separate Peace* by John Knowles: Allusions to this book are frequent in modern literature. It's also quite useful for learning the definition of "jounce."

*Adventure of Huckleberry Finn* by Mark Twain: The English language is continuously evolving. Read this for examples of words that no longer mean what they used to mean, except to SAT test makers.

*Brave New World* by Aldous Huxley: It's a much *happier* version of *1984*.

*Call of the Wild* by Jack London: It's an adventure story, really. Which means you can read it for fun.

*Catch 22* by Joseph Heller: How do you buy eggs for $3 and make a profit selling them for $2? Read *Catch 22* to find out! And a warning: there's quite a lot of adult material in the novel.

*Jane Eyre* by Charlotte Bronte: A dictionary is a must-have accompaniment to this novel. That, or the vocabulary list in this section. It's a tough read, but definitely worth finishing.

*Lord of the Flies* by William Golding: Reading this book with a British accent is advisable. It's the timeless story of a carefree group of English schoolchildren who create their own little dystopia on a deserted island.

*Lord of the Rings* by J.R.R. Tolkien: This series is my personal favorite. It is the greatest piece of fantasy literature I have ever consumed, and is a must read for fans of the imagination. *The Hobbit* is the prequel to the series, and is a terrific read as well.

*The Complete Works of William Shakespeare*: You ever get the feeling that some of the vocabulary you memorized have never be actually used in real life? Well, they get used here. Frequently.

*The Count of Monte Cristo* by Alexandre Dumas: This book is as exciting a novel as the canon of literature can produce. This book was also humorously alluded to in the movie *The Shawshank Redemption*.

*The Elements of Style*, by William Strunk and E.B. White: This book is commonly accepted as *the* guide to the English language. *Elements of Style* is a must read for anyone who seeks to write with skill.

*The Great Gatsby*: Here is one of the great American novels. It's also quite short, and I recommend it as a starter.

*The Inheritance Cycle* by Christopher Paolini : This quaternary is better known as the Eragon Series. It's rare for pop fiction for young adults to have impressive diction, but these books do.

*To Kill a Mockingbird* by Harper Lee: Lee's Atticus Finch is one of the most memorable characters in literature. He's also proven quite useful as an example for the SAT essay.

*Uncle Tom's Cabin* by Harriet Beecher Stowe: Lincoln once referred to this novel as the book that started the Civil War. It is the epitome of passionate writing, and will leave you in tears.

# How to Memorize Vocabulary

Memorizing the following list is definitely recommended. It's far less difficult than you would think, especially if you make a habit of it. I once tutored a violinist that memorized about 1000 new vocabulary words in 3 weeks. While not all of us can do that, tackling a few dozen a day, 5 or 6 days a week, is not difficult. Over time, that aggregates to a terrific vocabulary base.

To memorize large numbers of new words, it is best to use only simple definitions. Mentioning any one of these words should be able to prompt a synonym in your memory. (To see these words in action, make sure to read prolifically.) Writing and rewriting is a helpful memorization technique. Index cards can also be useful.

It's important to keep in mind that a word you just learned may not mean what you think it means. In essays, only use vocabulary that you have seen used before. For example, the word "fallow" in this list is defined as unused. However, "fallow" is used exclusively with farmland, so using it in the phrase, "this shiny wrench is fallow," would be quite improper.

# Grand Vocabulary List:

Assiduous: Hard Working
Aspersion: False rumor
Ascetic: Abstinent
Aesthetic: artistic
Arraign: A summon to court
Archaic: antique
Arable: farmable
Approbation: praise
Apotheosis: glorification
Apostate: One who changes his religion
Apocryphal: fake
Aphorism: old saying
Aphasia: mute
Antediluvian: prehistoric
Ancillary: accessory
Anathema: a curse
Amenity: pleasantness
Ambivalent: uncaring
Ampersand: the "&" symbol
Altercation: dispute
Assignation: assigned place
Atrophy: waste away
Attenuate: weaken
Augment: to enlarge
Augury: prophecy
Aural: related to hearing
Avarice: greed
Avuncular: like an uncle

Bedlam: a madhouse
Belie: to hide
Benighted: In the dark
Bestial: beastly
Bevy: group
Bilk: to obtain
Billet: barracks
Blandish: to flatter
Blithe: blissful
Broach: to mention
Bursar: treasurer


Calumny: false slander
Candor: honesty
Capitulate: to surrender
Carp: to scold
Catharsis: purification
Cavort: to frolic
Chary: watchful
Choleric: angry
Circumspect: cautious or suspicious
Clairvoyant: Has ESP
Clandestine: concealed
Cognomen: family name
Colloquial: informal/provincial
Collusion: work with
Commensurate: proportional
Complicity: accomplice
Conciliatory: overcoming distrust
Confection: sweet food
Confluence: joining place
Congenial: similar
Conglomerate: Mixture

Congruity: harmony
Consanguineous: Blood relation
Consummate: perfect
Continence: self control
Contrite: sorrowful
Convoluted: twisted
Coquette: a flirt
Corrugated: molded
Cosset: to pamper
Coterie: group
Craven: cowardly
Culmination: final stage
Cursory: superficial


Dearth: lack
Debauch: to corrupt
Debilitate: to weaken
Debunk: discredit
Debutante: ambitious female
Decry: belittle
Deferential: submissive
Defunct: dead
Deleterious: destructive
Delineation: representation
Demagogue: rabble rouser
Demarcation: borderline
Denigrate: to slander
Derogate: to belittle
Desiccated: dehydrated
Determinate: conclusive
Diatribe: verbal attack
Didactic: instructive
Diffidence: shyness

Digress: to stray
Dilatory: slow
Diluvia: flood
Dirge: funeral hymn
Discursive: wandering
Disparate: different
Dissemble: to pretend
Distend: to swell
Dither: confused
Diurnal: daily
Dogmatic: principled and stubborn
Dour: sullen
Dross: garbage
Duplicity: treachery
Dyspeptic: indigestion


Ebullient: exhilarated
Ecumenical: church related
Edify: to instruct
Efface: to erase
Efficacious: efficient
Effulgent: shining
Effluvia: outburst of gases
Effusive: emotional
Egregious: shockingly bad
Elicit: to provoke
Emend: to correct
Emollient: soothing
Endemic: inherent
Enervate: sap energy from
Ensconce: to settle
Ephemeral: fleeting
Epidermis: skin

Equanimity: calmness
Erudite: scholarly
Eschew: to avoid
Ethos: ethical beliefs
Euphony: harmony
Evanescent: momentary
Evince: to show
Exculpate: free from blame
Exigent: demanding
Expiate: to make amends
Expound: to elaborate on
Expunge: to erase
Extol: to praise


Facility: ease
Fallacious: false
Farcical: absurd
Fallow: unused
Fecund: fertile land
Felicitous: well spoken
Fiat: an arbitrary command
Fitful: irregular
Florid: gaudy
Foible: flaw
Foment: to incite
Forbearance: patience
Fracas: A fight
Frond: a leaf
Fulsome: scary
Furtive: secret: garner: to gather


Garrulous: talkative

Gnostic: related to knowledge
Gratis: free
Gustatory: related to taste


Hackneyed: worn out
Hegemony: rule, domination,
Hermetic: tightly sealed, waterproof
Heterodox: uncommon
Hidebound: stiff
Histrionic: overly emotional
Hutch: animal pen
Hyperbole: exaggeration


Ilk: a type
Impecunious: poor
Impertinent: rude
Implicit: not direct
Importune: to beg
Improvident: unplanned
Impudent: rude
Impugn: to challenge
Impute: to attribute to
Inane: futile, foolish
Incipient: initial
Inculcate: to teach
Incumbent: one who holds office
Indelible: permanent
Inebriated: drunk
Inexorable: unyielding
Inimical: hostile
Iniquity: a sin
Injunction: court order

Insipid: bland
Insolvent: bankrupt
Insular: isolated
Insuperable: unconquerable
Intemperate: not moderate
Inter: to bury
Interdict: to forbid
Intermittent: interrupted
Internecine: deadly
Interpolate: insert
Interregnum: interval between hegemonies
Intractable: difficult
Intransigent: uncompromising
Inundate: to submerge
Inure: to harden
Invective: a verbal assault
Investiture: investing in a person
Inveterate: confirmed
Invidious: obnoxious
Irascible: easily angered
Itinerant: wandering
Itinerary: plan or route


Jingoism: warmongering
Jubilee: celebration
Juncture: meeting point
Jurisprudence: philosophy of law
Juxtaposition: next to


Knoll: death bells

Lachrymose: fearful
Laconic: of few words
Lampoon: to mock
Lapidary: precious
Libertine: have no morals
Licentious: immoral
Liniment: medicine or bandages
Lissome: agile
Litigation: lawsuit
Loquacious: Talkative
Luscious: tasty


Machination: plan
Malapropism: misused word
Malinger: to fake illness
Manifold: diverse
Martinet: disciplinarian
Matriculate: to enter college
Mendacious: dishonest
Meretricious: gaudy
Militate: fight against
Misanthrope: one who hates humanity
Missive: a note
Moot: purely academic
Mores: morals
Moratorium: delay
Moribund: dying
Mottled: spotted
Munificent: generous
Myopic: nearsighted


Nadir: lowest point

Natal: birth related
Neonate: newborn
Nihilism: rejects principles
Nostalgia: love of the past
Novitiate: novice
Nuance: shade of meaning
Numismatic: related to coin collecting


Obdurate: stubborn
Obfuscate: to obscure
Obsequious: deferential
Obsequies: funeral rites
Obstinate: stubborn
Obstreperous: unruly
Obviate: to prevent
Occluded: isolated
Onerous: burdensome
Ontology: theory of existence
Opaque: abstruse
Opine: opinion related
Opprobrious: disgraceful
Oscillate: rock back and forth


Palatial: palace-like
Palaver: long talk
Palette: paint mixing board
Pall: lose interest
Palpable: obvious
Palpitation: shakes
Panache: flamboyance
Panegyric: elaborate
Panoply: impressive amount

Pare: to trim
Parity: equality
Parochial: of a limited scope
Parody: humorous imitation
Parsimony: stinginess
Pastiche: copied music
Pathos: compassion
Peccadillo: minor flaw
Pedagogue: teacher
Pedant: boring
Pejorative: verbal attack
Penchant: inclination
Penumbra: shadow
Penury: poverty
Perambulator: baby carriage
Perdition: damnation
Peregrinate: wandering
Perfidious: not loyal
Peripatetic: wandering eyes
Perjure: to lie in court
Perusal: examination
Philanderer: womanizer
Philology: study of words
Pious: devout
Pique: injured pride
Pithy: concise
Placid: calm
Plait: to braid
Platitude: a repeat
Pliant: yielding
Plucky: spunky
Pneumatic: related to air
Polemic: an argument

Polyglot: multilingual
Pontificate: to ramble
Portent: omen
Posterity: descendants
Potable: drinkable
Precept: law
Precipitous: hasty
Preclude: eliminate
Predicate: to base on
Preeminent: celebrated or famous
Preponderance: majority view
Presage: to foretell
Prescient: have foresight
Pretext an excuse
Prevaricate: to lie
Privation: loss of wealth
Probity: honesty
Profligate: corrupt
Profuse: to lavish out
Promontory: high ground
Promulgate: to make famous
Propensity: inclination
Propitiate: to win over
Propitious: favorable
Proponent: advocate of
Prosaic: common
Propinquity: nearness
Proselytize: to convert
Protagonist: main character
Protean: amorphous
Prude: civil
Prurient: lustful
Puerile: childish

Pugilism: boxing
Pugnacious: quarrelsome
Pulchritude: beauty
Purport: to claim


Quandary: a dilemma
Quaternary: 4 units
Quiescence: inactivity
Quixotic: impractical
Quotidian: daily


Raconteur: witty
Ramification: consequence
Rarefy: to purify
Ratiocination: logical
Rebut: to refute
Recalcitrant: rebel
Recant: to recall
Recapitulate: to review
Recondite: esoteric
Redress: relief
Refectory: dining room
Relegate: to assign
Rejoinder: a response
Remission: relaxation
Remit: to pay
Remuneration: wages
Renege: to break a promise
Repast: a meal
Repose: to relax
Repudiate: to reject
Requiem: funeral hymn

Rescind: to repeal
Reticent: reserved
Ribald: bawdy
Rife: widespread
Risqué: inappropriate
Rococo: ornamented
Rostrum: state


Saccharine: overly sweet
Sacrosanct: sacred
Sagacious: shrewd
Salient: jumping forth
Salubrious: healthy
Savant: learned person
Scrivener: copyist
Scurrilous: indecent
Sedentary: inactive
Seminal: related to beginnings
Senescent: aging
Sententious: moralizing
Seraphic: angelic
Sinecure: nominal job
Slough: to discard
Slovenly: messy
Sobriquet: nickname
Solecism: grammatical mistake
Solipsism: extreme narcissism
Sophist: orator
Soporific: sleepy
Sordid: filthy
Staid: restrained
Stand: group of trees
Stasis: motionless

Stigma: mark of shame
Stilled: stiff
Stint: amount of time
Stipend: allowance
Stricture: restraint
Strident: loud
Sublime: awe inspiring
Subpoena: A summon to court
Subterfuge: avoidance tactic
Subvert: to corrupt
Succinct: brief
Superannuated: archaic
Supercilious: haughty
Supplant: to substitute
Supplicant: a beggar
Surreptitious: secret
Swarthy: dark
Sybarite: pleasure seeker
Syllabus: outline
Symposium: meeting


Tableau: description
Tang: sharp taste
Tangential: diverting
Tawdry: gaudy
Tenable: defensible
Tenacious: stubborn
Tenet: belief
Tensile: durable
Terse: concise
Torpid: dormant
Transient: ephemeral
Transmute: to change

Travesty: sad parody
Trenchant: forceful
Trite: shallow
Tryst: romantic meeting
Turgid: swollen
Turpitude: vileness
Tyro: novice


Umbrage: verbal assault
Unctuous: greasy
Urbane: civil
Usury: banking
Utilitarian: efficient


Vaunted: flaunted
Venerable: respected due to age
Veracious: truthful
Verdant: full of plants
Verdure: vegetation
Verisimilitude: appearing to be true
Vernacular: related to language
Vernal: spring
Vestige: a remnant
Vicarious: a substitute
Vicissitude: changes
Vim: energy
Virile: manly
Viscous: syrupy
Vitriolic: bitter
Vituperate: to scold
Vociferous: loud
Voluble: glib

# Strategies

There are a few useful techniques to help you with your SAT reading passages.

For long passages, (30+ lines) always skim the questions before reading the passage. You're not skimming for content, but rather, for line numbers. Phrases like "between lines 35 and 47," and "the definition of the word in line 42," tell you what parts of the passage to read for detail. Mark up those lines before you start to read, then, once you've read a paragraph with marked lines, go back and answer the question. For short passages, you can skip right to the question.

Next, for "except" questions, it is necessary to find evidence in the passage to disprove all of the incorrect answers. For example, if the question states, "all of the following can be inferred from the passage *except,"* you must find evidence that four of the statements can be proven. Only then can you be sure that you have the right answer. With all other questions, you will also need to find evidence, though in those cases you will merely be looking for evidence that your chosen answer is correct.

In addition, putting your pencil on the text also helps improve reading speed. A landmark on the page can dramatically affect how quickly you read. Speed reading techniques like this can be mastered in less than 15 minutes.

For questions that ask for the tone or mood of the whole passage, it is helpful to read the first line of each of the paragraphs in the reading. This will usually give you the main idea of that the passage is about, without clouding your judgment with the little details.

Hardest of all is when you've narrowed the questions down to two answers. For these scenarios, it is more important than ever to go back to the text for support. Even if the questions is about mood or a general feelings, go back to the text for a word that would support the mood you choose.

Finally, remember to *read the words*. Everyone has had the experience of reading a passage, then looking back and remembering none of it. While reading, force yourself to pay attention to the text by summarizing as you read, and putting difficult sentences into your own words. All of this is done inside your head and takes little time, but that little time can be the difference between high quality recall and complete amnesia.

# Chapter 4: Math

## Algebra

Hopefully you are already familiar with the basics of algebra. You should be able to solve an algebraic function with one or two variables, and you should be able to convert word problems into numbers and variables. Here we will brush up on those two tasks.

We'll start easy:

Ex. 1) Given that $5x + 5 = 15$, what is the value of x?

A) 1
B) 2
C) 3
D) 4
E) 5

To solve this equation, we must isolate the x variable.

$5x + 5 = 15$
$5x = 10$
$x = 2$
The answer is B)

And that's all there is to it.

When given 2 equations, you can usually use substitution to solve for both variables.

Ex 2) If $5x + y = 20$ and $x + y = 8$, then what is $xy$?

A) 10
B) 15
C) 20
D) 25
E) 30

Let's isolate y first,

$x + y = 8$
$y = 8 - x$

Now we substitute that into the other given equation,

$5x + y = 20$
$5x + (8 - x) = 20$
$4x + 8 = 20$
$4x = 12$
$x = 3$

Now we substitute this value back into the first equation,

$x + y = 8$
$3 + y = 8$
$y = 5$

Finally, remember to obtain the value the question asked you for! In this case it's xy.

x = 3, y = 5
xy = 3(5)
xy = 15
The answer is B)

A final component of algebra is the skill of turning word problems into equations.

Ex 3. Pipe A can fill a tub in 3 hours. Pipe B can fill that same tub in 4 hours. Working together, how long does it take for the pipes to fill in the tub?

A) 99 minutes
B)110 minutes
C)103 minutes
D)1.72 minutes
E) 7 hours

So let's convert the question into equation form. "Pipe A can fill a tub in 3 hours." is the same as saying, "Pipe A can fill 1/3 of the tub per hour," or "Pipe A fills at the rate of one-thirds x, where x is time in hours."

Pipe A works at one-thirds x, where x is time in hours
Pipe A = x / 3

Using the same reasoning for " Pipe B can fill that same tub in 4 hours." we obtain:

Pipe B works at one-fourth x, where x is time in hours
Pipe B = x / 4

Therefore, when the pipes are working together, they work at the rate of pipe A + pipe B, or, x/3 + x/4. So how long does it get to get 1 full bathtub?

x/3 + x/4 = 1
0.333x + 0.25x = 1
0.583x = 1
x = 1.72 hours
x = 103 minutes

The answer is C) 103 minutes.

So that's algebra. Now, do a few hundred practice questions; since you have lots of time and dedication, that shouldn't be too much to ask for.

# Exponents

There are 5 basic rules of exponents that you need to memorize in order to be able to solve exponent questions on the SAT.

1) $x^a(x^b) = x^{a+b}$

$$\text{ex. } x^5 \, x^4 = x^{5+4} = x^9$$

2) $x^a / x^b = x^{a-b}$

$$\text{ex. } x^5 / x^4 = x^{5-4} = x^1$$

3) $(x^a)^b = x^{ab}$

$$\text{ex. } (x^5)^4 = x^{5*4} = x^{20}$$

4) $x^{-a} = 1 / x^a$

$$\text{ex. } x^{-5} = 1 / x^5$$

5) $x^0 = 1$

$$\text{ex. } 7^0 = 1$$

Now let's put these rules to the test.

Ex. 1 Simplify $x^{a-1}(x^{3a})(x^a)^2$

A) $x^{6a}$
B) $x^{6a+1}$
C) $x^{5a-12}$
D) $x^{6a-1}$
E) $x^6$

First we simplify each term in the expression. The first 2 terms are already in their simplest forms, but the last term can be simplified more with Rule 3.

$x^{a-1}(x^{3a})(x^a)^2$
$= x^{a-1}(x^{3a})(x^{2a})$

Next, we use Rule 1 to add up all of the exponents.

$x^{a-1}(x^{3a})(x^{2a})$
$= x^{a-1+3a + 2a}$
$= x^{6a-1}$

The answer is D) $x^{6a-1}$

Ex. 2 Simplify $x^{6a-1}(x^{-a})$

A)$x^{5a-1}$
B)$x^{6a+1}$
C)$x^{5a-12}$
D)$x^{6a-1}$
E)$x^{6}$

First we simplify all the terms in the expression. The first term has already been simplified, but the second needs some more work with Rule 4.

$$x^{6a-1}(x^{-a})$$
$$= x^{6a-1}(1/x^{a})$$
$$= x^{6a-1}/x^{a}$$

Now we use Rule 2 to simplify even further

$$x^{6a-1}/x^{a}$$
$$= x^{6a-1-a}$$
$$= x^{5a-1}$$

The answer is A) $x^{5a-1}$

As always, now you need to do a few hundred more exponents questions to truly master the subject.

# Functions

Functions questions are popular on the SAT math section.

Function notation questions usually look something like "f(x) = 2x + 3, solve for f(2)." The "f(2)" means to substitute "2" in for "x," and then solve. In this case, f(2) would equal 2(2) + 3, which is 7.

Any letter can be used in place of "f" and "x" with the same rules. You may be asked to find g(x) or even z(w). Just solve it as you would normally.

Ex. 1 $g(t) = 17t^2$, and $z(t) = 5t + 2$. find g(z(2))

A)342
B)2002
C)2844
D)2448
E)2428

Don't be intimidated by the double parentheses, that merely means "first find z(2), then find g( whatever z(2) came out to be). So let's start with z(2). When we substitute "2" in for "t" in the z(t) equation, we get 5(2) + 2, which is 12.

Then we find g(12). We substitute in "12" for "t" in the g(t) equation, and we get 17(144), which is 2448.

The answer is D) 2448.

Ex. 2 $f(x) = 7x^3$, and $z(x) = y$. find f(z(2))

A)56
B)$7y^3$
C)$7y$
D)7
E)$56y^3$

Here's a tricky question. z(x) actually does not depend on x, because no matter what you input for y the result will always be y. So, z(2) = y.

Now we substitute in "y" for "x" in f(x). We get that $f(x) = 7y^3$.

The answer is b) B)$7y^3$.

There are a variety of other functions questions on the SAT. Now it's up to you to try them all.

# Percents

You will definitely need to know you percentages for the SAT math section. They're not too difficult, once you get past the wording. You should already know how to convert among fractions, percentages, and decimals.

A few key ideas to remember for percent questions:

1. Raising an item's price 10% then lowering the price by 10% does not get you the initial value.

> ex. An $100 dress raised 10% becomes $110. An $110 dollar dress marked for 10% off becomes $99. 00 is not 100.

2. Raising an item's price by 10% (or 0.1) is the same as multiplying it by 1.1.

> ex. An $100 dress raised 7.3% (or 0.073) becomes 100 x 1.073 = $107.30 dollars.

3. Finding the percent of something simply means multiplying the something by the percent, then dividing by 100.

> ex. Find 3w percent of 12B

3w percent of 12B
= 3w (12B) / 100
= 36 wB / 100
= 9wB / 25

Great, now let's get started.

Ex. 1 The profit for Chen Incorporated was $400 million in its first year. Each year the profit is 10% higher than the previous year's profit. How much profit did Chen Incorporated obtain in its first 3 years?

A) $1.324 billion
B) $484 million
C) $1.324 million
D) $1.324
E) $4.84

We know that year one has a profit of $400 million, and that year two had 10% more than year one. Year two's profit is thus $400 million x 1.1 = $440 million.

Given that year two's profit is 440 million, and that year three's profit is 10% higher than year two's profit, we calculate year three's profit to be $440 million x 1.1 = $484 million.

We add the three profits up to obtain the total profit for the first three years.

$400 million + $440 million + $484 million
= $1324 million
= $1.324 billion

The answer is A) $1.324 billion

Ex. 2 An antiques price is raised 30%, then lowered 10%. What percent of its original value is the antique now worth?

A) 117
B) 117%
C) 1.17%
D) 120%
E) 80%

Let's substitute a value in for the price of the antique. Like $100.

So the antiques price is raised by 30%. That gets us $100 x 1.3 = $130.

It's next lowered by 10%, which brings the new price to 90% of the $130.
130 x 0.9 = $117.

What percent of $117 is $100? Let's find out by dividing the new price by the original price.

117 / 100
= 1.17 times the original value
= 117%

The answer is B) 117%

As always, now go practice a few hundred more questions.

# Permutations and Combinations

Permutations frequently show up in question 17 and question 18 on the SAT math section. Combinations are a rarity on the SAT, but are still useful to know. Overall, this is one of the harder topics in the SAT mathematics section. These questions ask you to find the number of ways to performs a certain task, like putting papers in a folder or forming student council committees from a class of many people.

The first thing to know is how to distinguish between permutations and combinations. Permutations are used when questions ask you for how many way to order things. The key word in there is "order." With permutations the order matters, like, "how many ways to order 10 people in a line of 7 people." (The remaining 3 people, we assume, is left out of the line.)

For combinations, the key words would be "committee," or "group." These questions look more like "how many committees of 7 can be formed from a group of 10 people?"

Let's solve these two questions. For the permutation one, we use the permutation formula of n! / (n-r)! Remember that since the question is about a situation where the order matters, we must use combinations.

What does the "!" mean? It means "Factorial." For example, "4!" is 4x3x2x1. "7!" is 7x6x5x4x3x2x1, "3!" is 3x2x1, and so on and so forth.

What about "n" and "r"? Simply put, n is the big number and r is the small number.

So let's go back to the question, "how many ways to order 10 people in a line of 7 people." 7 is the small number, 10 is the big number. So when we substitute in, we obtain:

n! / (n-r)!
=10! / (10-7)!
=10! / 3!
= 10x9x8x7x6x5x3x2x1 / 3x2x1


We can cancel out the "3x2x1" on the top and the bottom, to obtain 10x9x8x7x6x5x4, which is 564,800.


Now let's move to combinations. The combination formula is similar to the permutation formula, and looks like this:

$$\frac{n!}{(n-r)!(r!)}$$


So let's return to the question, "how many committees of 7 can be formed from a group of 10 people?"


n is still the big number, and 7 the small number. We substitute in and obtain:

$$\frac{10!}{(10-7)! \ (7!)}$$


We can simplify this.


$$\frac{10!}{3!7!}$$

Then,

10x9x8x7x6x5x4x3x2x1
3x2x1x7x6x5x4x3x2x1

The 7x6x5x4x3x2x1 cancels out, leaving

10 x 9 x 8
3 x 2 x 1

This simplifies to 120. There are 120 combinations.

Now let's try a few examples.

Ex.1 How many ways can I select a president, vice president, and secretary from a class of 8 students?

A) 120
B) 220
C) 320
D) 336
E)446

We use permutations for this question, because the order in which you select the officers matter. (Once you select a president, where are fewer people that are available to be vice president and secretary)

n! / (n-r)!
=8! / (8-3)!
=8! / 5!
= $\frac{8x7x6x5x4x3x2x1}{5x4x3x2x1}$

= 8x7x6
=336

The Answer is D) 336 ways

Ex. 2 How many ways are there to select a committee of 3 officers from a class of 8 students?

A)336
B)112
C) 56
D) 244
E) 8

Now we move to combinations, since we are looking for a committee.

$$\frac{n!}{(n-r)!(r!)}$$

$$\frac{8!}{(8-3)!\ (3!)}$$

Which becomes

$$\frac{8!}{5!3!}$$

Then,

$$\frac{8 \times 7 \times 6 \times 5 \times 4 \times 3 \times 2 \times 1}{3 \times 2 \times 1 \times 5 \times 4 \times 3 \times 2 \times 1}$$

Then,

$$\frac{8 \times 7 \times 6}{3 \times 2 \times 1}$$

This simplifies to 56.

The answer is C) 56 ways.

Notice that there are always fewer combinations than permutations. That's because when order doesn't matter, all of the repeats get eliminated. For example, the arrangement "A, B, C" and "B, A, C" count as 2 ways in a permutation question, but just 1 way in a combination question.

Now practice!

# Probability

Let's first review the basics of probability.

Probability is usually measured with fractions. What are the odds of getting heads on a fair coin? 1/2. What are the odds of getting a 6 when rolling a fair die? 1/6.

Occasionally, you will have to do a lot of listing when asked to perform probability questions. What is the probability of getting a 5 when you toss 2 dice? List the probabilities: 1 and 4, 2 and 3, 3 and 2, 4 and 1. This is four ways out of 6x6=36 possible combinations. 4/36 = 1/9.

Hopefully you could follow all that. If not, you are seriously behind in elementary probability. I would recommend consulting some local library books on fundamentals of probability if that is the case.

Anyways, SAT probability hinges around these fraction problems, and 2 words: "and," and "or." The simple rule of thumb is that when a question asks you to find the probability of this *and* that happening, you multiply fractions, and when a question asks you to find the probability of this *or* that happening, you add fractions.

Let's take a look at a few examples.

Ex. 1 When you throw 2 fair die, what are the odds of getting a sum that is a prime number?

A)1/2
B)5/11
C)1/4
D)9/36
E) 5/12

First, let's have a quick refresher on prime numbers. They're the ones with no multiples other than 1 and the number itself. Remember that 1 is not a prime number. The primes that we can produce with 2 dice are always under 12, since 6+6 is 12. Those primes are 2, 3, 5, 7, and 11.

We convert this question into "and/or" format. What the question really is asking is, "what is the probability of getting a 2, 3, 5, 7, or 11 when 2 dice are thrown." The key word here is "or", and it tells us to add the fractions. So we find the probability of getting each of those numbers, and then add them up.

Ways to get a sum of 2: rolling a 1 and 1. One Way = 1/36 chance of rolling a 2.
Ways to get a sum of 3: rolling a 2 and 1, rolling a 1 and 2. Two ways = 2/36 chance of rolling a 3.
Ways to get a sum of 5: rolling a 1 and 4, rolling a 2 and 3, rolling a 3 and 2, rolling a 4 and 1. Four ways = 4/36 chance of getting a 5
Ways to get a sum of 7: rolling a 1 and 6, rolling a 2 and 5, rolling a 3 and 4, rolling a 4 and 3, rolling a 5 and 2, rolling a 6 and 1. Six ways = 6/36 chance of getting a 7.
Ways to get a sum of 11: rolling a 5 and 6, rolling a 6 and 5. Two ways = 2/36 chance of getting an 11.

Adding up the fractions gets us $1/36 + 2/36 + 4/36 + 6/36 + 2/36 = 15/36 = 5/12$.

The answer is E) 5/12

Ex. 2 A room contains 10 women and 9 men. Three people are picked at random. What are the odds that they are all men?

A) 28/323
B) 42/433
C) 9/19
D) 8/18
E) 7/17

Once again, we need to convert the question into and/or format. The question is really asking us, "what is the probability of selecting a man and then selecting another man and then selecting another man?"

So what are the odds of selecting a man? At the beginning it is 9 men out of a total of 19 people, so the fraction is 9/19. Next, with 1 man gone, the probability of selecting another man is 8/18. Then 7/17. Since the question is an "and" question, we multiply the fractions together.

9/19 x 8/18 x 7/17 = 504/5814 = 28/323.

The answer is A) 28/323

As always, now you need to practice a lot more questions.

# Proportions

Proportions are quite common on the SAT, and come in a variety of forms.

The simplest proportions can be solved using basic algebra. A one-variable equation can account for the easy direct ratio questions.

Ex.1 The ratio of red marbles to blue marbles in a bucket is 4:5. There are a total of 180 marbles in the bucket. How many marbles are blue?

A) 60
B) 70
C) 80
D) 90
E) 100

Let's start by putting the problem into equation form. There are 4x blue marbles in that bucket, and 5x red marbles in the bucket. We also know that there is a total of 180 marbles in the bucket.

$4x + 5x = 180.$
$9x = 180$
$x = 20$

Great! Now remember that we are asked to find the number of blue marbles. That's 5x marbles, as we defined earlier.

$5x = 5(20) = 100$

There are 100 blue marbles. The answer is E) 100.

Occasionally, the question presents an inverse ratio question. To deal with inverse variation, a slightly different algebraic equation needs to be used.

Ex. 2 If 4 drainage pipes can empty a tub in 8 hours, then how long will it take to empty the tub when 6 drainage pipes are used?

A) 3 hours
B) 2 hours
C) 160 minutes
D) 320 minutes
E) 640 minutes

First, let's identify why the question is an inverse relation question. Logically, the more drainage pipes there are, the less time it takes to drain the tub, right? There more, the more of 1 variable (pipe) there is, the less of another variable (time) there is. That's a inverse situation.

For inverse situations, multiplication is used. Think of the tub as needing a certain number of pipe-hours to drain. 4 pipes x 8 hours = 32 pipe-hours.

4 pipes (8 hours) = 6 pipes (x hours)
32 = 6x
x = 5.33333 hours
x = 320 minutes

The answer is D) 320 minutes.

# Quadratic Equations

The main reason you to bring a graphing calculator to the SAT instead of a basic 4 function is to graph quadratic equations. But to be able to make use of your calculator, first you must know how recognize information from a graph.

Quadratic equations are usually graphed in the form:

$$y = a \, (x-h)^2 + k$$

If "a" is positive, the graph opens up. If it's negative, the graph opens down. The "h" value determines left to right movement, and the "k" value determines up and down movement. Let's see this in action.

a) This is the graph of $y = x^2$. It is the parent equation of all other quadratic equations

b) This is the graph of $y = (x-2)^2$, notice that because the h value is 2, the graph has moved 2 units to the right.

c) This is the graph of $y = (x-2)^2 + 3$, notice because the h value is 2, the graph has moved 2 units to the right, and that because the k value is 3, the graph has moved 3 units upwards.

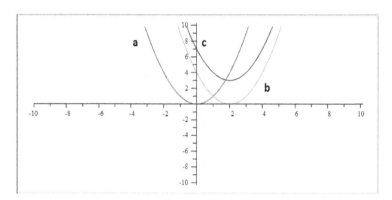

Now let's move to the real questions.

Ex. 1 Which of the following could be the equation of figure a shifted 3 units up?

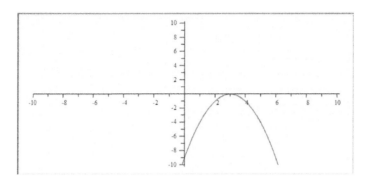

Figure A

A) $(x-2)^2$
B) $(x-2)^2 + 3$
C) $-(x-2)^2 + 2$
D) $-(x-3)^2 + 3$
E) $-(x-2) + 3$

Let's examine the graph. From the parent equation of $y = x^2$, it is shifted 3 units to the right, and flipped upside-down. This tells us that the a value is negative, and that the h value is 2. Thus, we conclude the equation shown is $y = -(x-3)^2$

In order to move that equation up 3 units, we change the k value to 3. Thus we are left with the equation $-(x-3)^2 + 3$. The answer is D).

Occasionally, other forms of quadratics questions will also show up. Practice hundreds more questions to catch them all!

# Series

Most of the time, you'll be using substitution and guess and check to solve questions involving series, but it's useful to be prepared for when you need the series formula.

Geometric series (ones that involve multiplication) do not show up on the SAT, so you will not need to know the formula for geometric series.

For arithmetic series (ones that involve addition), the formula is

$$\text{Sum} = n\ (a_1 + a_n)\ /\ 2$$

"n" is the number of numbers you are adding, $a1$ is the first number you want to add, and $an$ is the last number you want to add. So if I wanted to add all the numbers between 1 and 50, I would substitute 50 into n, "1" into $a1$ and 50 into an.

$$50[(1+50)/\ 2] = 1275$$

And there you have it; the sum of 1 to 50 is 1275

Ex. 1 Five consecutive positive integers add up to 60. What is the greatest of the integers?

A) 10
B) 13
C) 14
D) 18
E) 60

We substitute the given values into the series equation. 60 is the sum and n is 5 because there are 5 numbers. The difference between a1 and anis 4 numbers, so we can set $a_1$ as x and $a_n$ as x+4

$60 = 5 [(x + x+4)/2]$
$12 = (x + x+4)/2$
$24 = x + x+4$
$24 = 2x + 4$
$20 = 2x$
$x = 10$

So now we know that $a_1$ is 10. That makes the series of numbers 10, 11, 12, 13, 14. We are asked to find the greatest in that series of numbers. 14 is the greatest number, so the answer is C) 14.

Remember that sometimes, you can also just guess and check to find the answer. Given that the sum is 60, you could have estimated the series of 5 numbers to be in the tens, eventually stumbled upon the right series. This method can be just as effective in the proper situation. To master which method to use, go and practice a few hundred more questions!

# Statistics

Mean, median, mode. Hopefully you've been hearing about these for a few years now. Let's quickly review what they are.

The mean is simply the average of all of the numbers in a group of numbers. So let's take the set of numbers, {2, 4, 5, 6, 6, 6, 9}. When you add up all the numbers and divide by the total number of numbers, you get 5.43. That's the mean.

The median is the number that is in the exact middle of the set. In this case it's 6.

The mode is the value that occurs the most frequently in the set. The number 6 appears 3 times, and therefore it is the mode.

Ex. 1 Daniel's SAT class of 10 students has averaged a score improvement of 200 points. A new student takes the SAT and afterwards the average score improvement is 210 points. How many points did the new student improve his score by?

A) 300
B) 310
C) 330
D)400
E) 440

This question deals with averages, so we need to use the mean.

Let's first turn the question into equation form. "Class of 10 students has averaged a score improvement of 200 points," means that for all intents and purposes, we can assume every student's improvement was 200.

10 x 200 = 2000

In total, the students improved 2000 points.

Once the new student takes the test, the average comes out to 210. That means the 2000 points that we already have, plus the new students score "x", divided by the total of 11 students, gives us the average of 210.

$(2000 + x) / 11 = 210$

$2000 + x = 2310$

$x = 310$ points

The answer is B) 310

Ex. 2 The highest and lowest values in a set of 11 numbers are removed. Which of the following definitely have not been affected?

I. The mean
II. The median
III. The mode

A) I only
B) II only
C) III only
D) I and II
E) I, II, and III

97

This is a conceptual question, and yes, they do appear on the SAT math section. We need to imagine scenarios where we can eliminate choices.

If the series consisted of mostly single digit numbers, and one 5 digit number, then the mean would be a pretty large number. (At least 4 digits) By removing the highest and lowest number, the mean would become a single digit number. It would change significantly, and so we eliminate I, and any answer that mentions I.

If the highest number is the mode, and only appears twice, then we have removed the mode of the set of values. The mode would thus have been affected, and we eliminate II.

However, since the median is the middle value in the set, removing the top and bottom value would still leave it in the middle. It is not affected. II is the only viable choice.

The answer is B) II only.

# Triangles

Knowing your triangle fundamentals is crucial on the SAT math section. For examples, you should definitely remember that all the angles in a triangle add up to 180 degrees. SAT math sometimes goes more in depth with triangles though.

Two types of special triangle are the 30-60-90 triangle and the 45-45-90 triangle. These two types of triangles always retain certain ratios of side length.

In the 30-60-90 triangle, the shortest side is always across from the angle with 30 degrees. The longest side, the hypotenuse, is always twice the length of the shortest side. The remaining side, the one across from the 60 degrees angle, is always $\sqrt{3}$ times the length of the shortest side.

For example, if we are given that the length of the longest side is x, we can find the lengths of the other 2 sides. The shortest side, which is half as long as the longest, would be x/2 units long. The other side, which is $\sqrt{3}$ times as long as the shortest side, would be $(x\sqrt{3})/2$ units long.

Next let us examine the 45-45-90 triangle. Since it is an isosceles triangle, the 2 legs are the same length. The hypotenuse is always 2 times the length of the legs.

For example, if we are given that the length of the longest side is x, we can find the lengths of the two legs. Since the hypotenuse is 2 times as long as the legs, the legs are thus 1/2 the length of the hypotenuse. The length of the legs would be x/2 units long.

Ex. 1 Given an equilateral triangle with all sides length "a", what would be the height of the triangle?

A) $2a\sqrt{3}/2$
B) $a\sqrt{3}$
C) $a/2$
D) $a\sqrt{3}/2$
E) $3a\sqrt{2}/2$

We can break an equilateral triangle down into two 30-60-90 triangles. When given that information, the rest of the problem becomes easy.

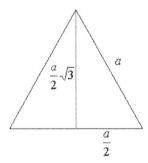

Now that we are looking at two 30-60-90 triangles, we can easily identify that the height of the original triangle is the side of a 30-60-90 triangle that faces the 60side, which is $a\sqrt{3}/2$. The answer is D) $a\sqrt{3}/2$.

Ex. 2 What is the perimeter of a 45-45-90 triangle, given that the hypotenuse is y?

A) $y^2$
B) $y + y\sqrt{2}$
C) $y\sqrt{2} + 2$
D) $2y$
E) $2$

This is another basic question with the special triangles.

Since the hypotenuse is length y, then the legs must be length $y/\sqrt{2}$. The perimeter is thus:

$$y + (y / \sqrt{2}) + (y / \sqrt{2})$$
$$= y + (2\,y / \sqrt{2})$$
$$= y + 2y\sqrt{2}/2$$
$$= y + y\sqrt{2}$$

The answer is B) $y + y\sqrt{2}$ . Remember to avoid leaving a radical in the denominator!

Now get some more practice with these triangles.

# Venn Diagrams

Venn Diagrams are a useful tool on the SAT. The one rule of Venn diagram drawing is to start in the middle. From there, simple math can help you figure out the rest of the question.

Ex. 1 A group of 50 students have 30 math students, 25 English students, and 18 students who take math and English. How many students take neither math nor English?

A) 9
B) 10
C) 11
D) 12
E) 13

First we need to find out how many students participate in each activity. We start with a simple Venn diagram. Remember to fill in the center value first, which in this case is 18. (Because 18 students are in both categories.

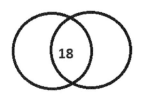

We define the right side to be the math side and the left side to be the English side. There are 30 total math students, so 30-18 gives us 12 students who only take math. There are 25 total English students, so

25-18 gives us 7 students who only take English. We fill that information in.

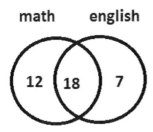

The total number of students in here is 12+18+7, which gives us 37 students who take math, English, or math and English. This also means that 50-37=13 students taken neither math nor English. The answer is E) 13.

When dealing with more than two categories, the rules remain the same. First fill in the center, then work your way out.

Now that you've worked with the harder Venn diagrams, you should be ready to take on any Venn diagram question you can come across! Go practice your new skill!

# Chapter 5: The Ten Week Plan

## SAT Practice Schedule

Perhaps you picked up this book 2 months before your SAT exam. That's perfectly alright. 10 weeks is still enough time to significantly improve your SAT score. Here is the lesson plan that I use with all of my students. Much of the material that I refer to can be found in Chapter 2 of this book, but you will need to obtain additional resources and test compilations.

**Week 1:**

Reading:

1) Read Chapter 2's discussion on a proper SAT essay. Memorize the SAT Essay Structure.

Homework:

1) Memorize 20 SAT Words from the Grand Vocabulary List.
2) Complete 2 practice essays using the SAT Essay Structure
3) Practice a section of passage reading from an additional practice test compilation.

**Week 2:**

Reading:

1) Read grammar rules 1-8 from the Writing section.
2) Read a news article from a respected newspaper or magazine and write a practice essay using the article as one of your examples. This will get you in the habit or finding quality examples to use in your SAT Essay.

Homework:

1) Write 3 practice essays with proper structure
2) Memorize 20 SAT words
3) Practice a section of passage reading from an additional practice test compilation.

## Week 3

Reading:

1) Finish reading the grammar section
2) Select a book from the suggested readings list and read the first 100 pages.

Homework:

1) Complete the grammar drills
2) Complete 3 practice essays using proper structure
3) Memorize 25 SAT words

## Week 4

Vocabulary Quiz

1) Quiz yourself on the words you have memorized in the first 3 weeks.

Reading:

1) Read the discussion on Passage Reading Questions.
2) Continue your reading book

Homework:

1) Grammar Practice: Complete 1 Writing section from a practice SAT
2) Complete 3 more practice essays using proper Structure
3) Memorize 25 SAT words
4) Reading practice: complete 1 Reading section from a practice SAT

## Week 5

Reading:

1) Math Lesson I: Algebra and Exponents
2) Finish your first reading book

Homework:

1) Complete 3 essays using proper structure
2) Grammar Practice: complete 1 Writing section from a practice SAT
3) Reading Practice: Complete 1 Reading section from a practice SAT
4) Memorize 25 SAT words

## Week 6

Vocabulary Quiz

1) Quiz yourself on all of the vocabulary you have memorized since week 1

Reading:

1) Math Lesson II: Functions and Percents
2) Select another title from the Suggested Reading list and read the first 100 pages.

Homework:

1) Complete 1 full practice SAT test. Correct each section after you complete it instead of waiting for the whole test to be finished. Return to each incorrect answer and fix it afterwards.
2) Memorize 25 SAT words

## Week 7

Reading

1) Math Lesson 3:  Permutations and Combinations, Probability
2) Continue reading your title from the Suggested Readings list.

Homework

1) Complete and correct 2 full practice tests
2) Memorize 30 SAT words

## Week 8

Reading:

1) Math Lesson IV: Proportions, Quadratics, and Series
2) Finish your book from the Suggested Readings list.

Homework:

1) Complete and correct 2 full practice tests
2) Memorize 30 SAT words

## Week 9

Reading:

1) Math Lesson V: Statistics, Triangles, Venn Diagrams

Homework

1) Complete and correct 2 full practice tests
2) Memorize 30 SAT words

## Week 10

Grand Vocabulary Quiz

1) Quiz yourself on all of the vocabulary you have memorized the past 10 weeks.

Homework:

1) Complete and correct 2 full SAT practice tests
2) Memorize 25-30 SAT words

After these 10 weeks of practice, you should be all set to take the SAT with the expectation of a 2200, or 200 points of improvement from your last SAT. Good Luck!

# Chapter 6: Final Comments

## Day of the Exam

### Last Minute Preparation

As you have no doubt heard before, the most important task you can do the night before the exam is sleep. It'll do wonders for you.

However, once you've allocated for yourself enough hours for that, you may have an hour or two left over. In that time, it's helpful to go over the grand conceptual topics. Review the grammar rules, but don't actually practice any questions. Review the essay structure, but there's no need to write any more essays. Review the math formulas, and... well, do a *little* practice if you're feeling up to it. Overall, there's no more need to cram in any extra studying. Hopefully one night's worth of hours won't matter at all in the grand total of the number of hours you've studied.

Avoid any parties or celebrations the night before, or anything too exciting for that matter. According to psychology's Arousal Theory, the best state to be in before an event like the SAT is moderately excited. So make sure you aren't too tired or too excited the day of the exam. Also avoid any so-called brain enhancement drugs. They do nothing for you.

Oh yeah, and remember to breathe!

# Special Testing Months

A common misconception about the SAT is that there are certain months that have "better" curves and thus easier tests. I've heard countless theories on taking the SAT in May when all the AP kids are too busy with AP exams, or taking the test in September so there are lots of "slacker" seniors bringing the curve down.

Unfortunately, there are no special months or super-curve tests. The factors all balance out. The Perfect Score Project has an excellent table of SAT test curves by month for several years, and after I ran a few chi square tests on the data, there was no statistical significance. That means there is no real evidence of any correlation between curves and test month. That also means there is no disadvantageous month for taking the SAT.

That being said, the placebo effect can also perform wonders. Studies and psychology textbooks have both stated that at times it works even as well as psychotherapy. So if it makes you feel better to believe that your test month is a "curve" month, go right ahead. Your score will likely be higher because you want it to be.

The most important idea to take away from this though, is that your SAT score will eventually depend on you. It's your hard work that's going to get for yourself improvement and Ivy League scores. So practice!

# Super Scores

Some colleges will allow you to "Super-score" your SAT score by taking only your best Reading, Writing, and Math scores from separate tests. Definitely make sure to check if the colleges you are applying to allow super-scores.

Most Ivy League colleges, however, will not allow you to super-score your tests. Applicants have to submit the score of all of the SATs you've ever taken, and are not allowed to pick and choose the best scores from several attempts. So remember to always take the entire test seriously, even if you're only aiming to improve a writing score.

# Subject Tests

Those of you that like to plan ahead may already be thinking about the subject tests. I obtained a perfect score on four of those too, so I feel I'm qualified to give a few tidbits of advice.

First off: don't take three tests at once. Studying for three at once divides your attention, and taking three at once just makes you plain tired. The only SAT exam I've ever retaken was an "exam 3," and when I took it by itself the perfect score fell right in my lap. Besides, most colleges only want two exams anyways.

Also, try to take exams that you will perform well on. That means avoiding the Chinese subject test, (it's full of native speakers that ruin the curve and raise the difficulty) and sticking to your strengths.

Finally, try to pick tests that will be useful in college. My Literature subject test ended up being absolutely worthless, whereas my science SATs allowed me to place out of intro classes. A good score on an hour long subject test may even exempt you from having to take a three hour long AP exam.

For now though, focus on the SAT.

CPSIA information can be obtained at www.ICGtesting.com
Printed in the USA
BVOW11s1117020314

346333BV00013B/249/P

9 781494 227913